P9-CCS-370

FAMOUS MOVIE MONSTERS™

MEET

GODZILLA

The Rosen Publishing Group, Inc.
New York

ROBERT GREENBERGER

For Robbie

Published in 2005 by the Rosen Publishing Group, Inc.
29 East 21st Street, New York, NY 10010

Library of Congress Cataloging-in-Publication Data

Greenberger, Robert.
Meet Godzilla/Robert Greenberger.– 1st ed.
    p. cm—(Famous movie monsters)
Includes filmography.
Includes bibliographical references and index.
ISBN 1-4042-0269-2
1. Godzilla films—History and criticism—Juvenile literature.
I. Title. II. Series.
PN1995.9.G63G74 2005
791.43'651—dc22

2004008426

Manufactured in the United States of America

On the cover: Godzilla terrorizes Tokyo with his radioactive breath.

CONTENTS

CHAPTER 1

THE COMING OF GODZILLA

American newspaper reporter Steve Martin, in a voice-over narration, explains, "This is Tokyo, once a city of 6 million people. What has happened here was caused by a force which up until a few days ago was entirely beyond the scope of man's imagination. Tokyo—a smoldering memorial to the unknown, an unknown which at this very moment still prevails and could at any time lash out with its terrible destruction anywhere else in the world."

Martin lies buried beneath the rubble of the news building in downtown Tokyo, Japan. He tries to free himself from the rubble, but he is weak from his injuries and collapses. When he awakens, he is being carried by medics through the ward of a hospital where hundreds of people lie wounded, dying, or dead. Martin recognizes his friend Emiko Yamane, who has volunteered as a nurse to help with the city's horrific devastation. Emiko tries to comfort Steve, and he asks her whether her father, Dr. Kyohei Yamane, has

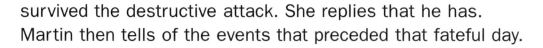

survived the destructive attack. She replies that he has. Martin then tells of the events that preceded that fateful day.

* * *

Steve Martin is on an assignment for *United World News* and is headed to Cairo, Egypt. He decides to stop off in Tokyo to visit his college friend, Dr. Daisuke Serizawa. When he gets off the airplane in Tokyo, Martin learns that Serizawa has to attend a meeting and cannot meet him. Security officer Tomo Iwanaga asks Martin if he noticed anything peculiar during the flight. While being questioned, Martin learns that below the airplane's flight path, a ship sailing on the ocean was mysteriously set on fire.

* * *

The crewmen aboard a boat of the Nanking Shipping Company relax on the water. Music drifts lazily through the air. Everything changes in an instant as a blinding flash of light disrupts the mood. One crewman looks over the side of the boat and is stunned to see the nearby water boiling. Then there's a second flash of light. The crewmen cover their eyes, and the boat is engulfed in a ball of fire. A radio operator sends out a Mayday message before the boat is destroyed.

* * *

Martin shows security officer Iwanaga his press identification and asks if he can learn more about the ship's demise. Martin finds out that a total of eight fishing boats around Japan have been destroyed, going up in flames, killing almost everyone aboard. All the boats report a roar and a blinding flash of light before their radios go silent. One might be written off as an accident, but when the pattern repeats itself for days, it causes alarm among Tokyo's inhabitants. A sense of concern is raised by the military and medical personnel, who hope to uncover the cause of these problems before the shell-shocked populace is thrown into a panic. Martin calls his home office and gets permission to stay in Japan to cover the story.

Survivors of a shipwreck wash ashore on tiny Odo Island in the Pacific Ocean. Several die before proper medical treatment can be administered, but they, too, speak of the blinding light. The island's villagers look at one another knowingly.

When word reaches the mainland that there are survivors and that the islanders believe the cause of the destruction is from a living being, a research team is dispatched to Odo Island. Leading the group is renowned paleontologist Dr. Kyohei Yamane. Yamane's daughter, Emiko, security officer Iwanaga, and Steve Martin accompany the scientists.

When the group arrives on the island, one of the villagers explains to Dr. Yamane that their legends tell of a dangerous creature, a monster that lives in the waters near the island. They fear that this beast, known as Godzilla (*Gojira* in Japanese [go-JEER-a, a combination of the English word "gorilla" and the Japanese word *kujira*, meaning "whale"]), has awakened.

That night, Martin's group watches a native ceremony that recounts an ancient ritual in which the villagers sent young women out to sea on a raft as a sacrifice to Godzilla. After the dance, Martin and Iwanaga head for their tents to go to sleep. A sudden tropical storm darkens the skies and whips the people with wind and rain. Martin and Iwanaga hold fast to the trunk of a tree so they will not be blown away. In the aftermath, Yamane studies the destruction, ascribing it to the storm, not to a monster.

Some of the islanders are taken to the mainland to tell their story to the authorities. The islanders believe that Godzilla is the cause of all the destruction. Dr. Yamane volunteers to return to Odo Island for further studies.

Martin again accompanies the scientists, and he notices that Emiko and a young naval officer, Hideto Ogata, spend much time together. When they reach the island, Dr. Yamane and the others investigate the villages that have been destroyed. Another scientist uses a Geiger counter and detects higher than normal radiation near the damaged structures. The readings are alarming enough that Dr. Yamane warns the villagers not to drink the water. The scientists then stumble across another radioactive hot spot, which is revealed as a giant footprint. Clearly, some living being has caused the problems—could it be the islanders' monster? Dr. Yamane also discovers a trilobite, a marine animal from the Paleozoic period, which was thought to have been extinct. It's also obvious that the villagers are in danger of radiation poisoning and must leave the island.

Before leaving, Dr. Yamane and his group decide to take more readings, but they are startled by the ringing of a giant bell. Villagers hurry past them, and they conclude that the bell is a warning. They look up and get their first glimpse of a tall, gray-skinned creature. Godzilla is atop a hill. Even from a distance, the tall dinosaur-like monster is imposing. Photographs are taken to prove the creature's existence.

Ogata (Akira Takarada), Masaji (Ren Yamamoto), Gisaku (Kokuten Kodo), Emiko (Momoko Kochi), Yamane (Takashi Shimura), and Serizawa (Akhiko Hirata) catch a glimpse of the giant monster. Director Ishiro Honda originally wanted Godzilla to make his first appearance with a bloody cow in his mouth. However, he felt the scene didn't look right, so he reshot the sequence without the cow.

The scientists take some of the islanders to Tokyo, and at a hastily arranged press conference, Dr. Yamane explains his belief that the recent American testing of hydrogen bombs may have awakened Godzilla. The fallout from the tests may also have mutated the creature into being radioactive, presenting an even greater danger to life. Yamane insists that the creature must be studied, not killed. He is opposed not only by Emiko, but even Ogata. Dr. Yamane argues that if Godzilla could survive something as powerful as a hydrogen bomb, how could the military try to stop him? Instead, by studying the creature, he argues, they may learn useful ways of protecting humankind from radiation.

After Dr. Yamane's address, Martin phones his friend Serizawa to find out whether they can meet that evening. Serizawa replies that he already has plans to meet with Emiko but that he and Martin can meet on the following day.

Shortly thereafter, Emiko visits Serizawa. Although they've been engaged since they were children, Emiko wants to tell Serizawa that she really doesn't love him, and that she loves Hideto Ogata instead. Before she can reveal the reason for her visit, Serizawa grabs her wrist and takes her to his laboratory. There, with a mixture of pride and apprehension, he unveils his invention, the Oxygen Destroyer, a device that is able to dissolve the molecular bonds between oxygen and hydrogen in water. This chemi cal process could destroy native sea life, and Serizawa, a pacifist, fears if anyone learns of it, it would become a tool of the military. He swears Emiko to secrecy, and she keeps not only his secret but her own.

A day later, the Japanese defense force decides to send a naval vessel out into the ocean to fire depth charges where it believes Godzilla is resting. The massive explosions that the sailors hear lead them to conclude that they are victorious in killing the creature. As the ship's crew heads back to port, no one notices Godzilla's head breaking the surface and watching the vessel.

Serizawa reveals his invention to Emiko but swears her to secrecy. The actors in this scene, Akhiko Hirata (*right*) and Momoko Kochi, both appeared in subsequent Godzilla films for Toho.

As the citizens of Tokyo celebrate the quick end to the threat, a roar is heard across the city. People near the docks watch in terror as Godzilla, as tall as a thirty-storied building, comes ashore and destroys the docks, several buildings, and an elevated train. Military forces mobilize and then fire at the monster, but their bullets have no effect. Godzilla returns to the water and escapes unharmed.

Martin asks Iwanaga if anything can be done to stop Godzilla. Iwanaga shows Martin how the military is fortifying the city by erecting huge high-tension electric lines. The defense force then herds the populace behind the humming barrier. Godzilla emerges once more and walks through countless volts of energy. Godzilla wreaks more havoc on the city and blasts Tokyo with his radioactive breath. Meanwhile Martin, back in the news building, describes Godzilla's movements while speaking into his tape recorder. The monster reaches the news building and quickly demolishes it. Martin is left buried in the rubble. A jet squadron manages to lead Godzilla away from the nearly ravaged Tokyo, back into Tokyo Bay.

*   *   *

Ogata joins Emiko at Martin's bedside in the hospital. Tired of feeling helpless, Emiko finally breaks down and tells Ogata and Martin about Serizawa's device. Martin pleads with Emiko and Ogata to convince Serizawa that he must use the Oxygen Destroyer against Godzilla.

Emiko and Ogata visit Serizawa and ask him for the weapon. "If the Oxygen Destroyer is used even once," Serizawa argues with his fiancée and the naval man, "politicians from around the world will see it. Of course they'll use it as a weapon. Bombs versus bombs, missiles versus missiles, and now a new super-weapon to throw upon us all. As a scientist, no, as a human being, I cannot allow that to happen." The highly moral doctor refuses even to consider their request until he sees a television broadcast of Godzilla's destructive visit to Tokyo. Morality is important to Serizawa,

but clearly Godzilla must be stopped before all Japanese life is destroyed. Serizawa reluctantly agrees that the Oxygen Destroyer will only be used this one time. Serizawa burns the plans of his work and destroys his lab. He explains, "Humans are weak animals. Even if I burn my notes, the secret will still be in my head. Until I die, how can I be sure I won't be forced by someone to make the device again?"

Serizawa insists he must be there to activate the device, trusting no one, not even as honest a man as Ogata. They agree to go together to save Tokyo.

The next day, Serizawa and Ogata don scuba gear and dive deep into Tokyo Bay to place the Oxygen Destroyer near Godzilla. Once the device is in position, Ogata returns to the surface, but Serizawa stays underwater and cuts his oxygen tube. Running out of air, Serizawa triggers the device and it works as expected. The oxygen is burned off, the sea churns, and Godzilla writhes in pain and makes his way to the surface. Godzilla emerges once, gives a final defiant roar and then sinks, his hide beginning to dissolve.

Martin says that the world has lost a great man in Serizawa but that it will be able to live to see tomorrow because of him. People turn their attentions to salvaging their city. The rebuilding of Tokyo can begin along with the blossoming romance of Ogata and Emiko.

Godzilla breathes atomic fire on the citizens of Tokyo. Godzilla's Japanese name, Gojira, is a combination of the words "gorilla" and "kujira" (whale). It was originally a nickname given to a press agent for Toho who was very large in size.

CHAPTER 2

GOJIRA, *THE MAKING OF A MODERN MYTH*

A big-budget coproduction between an Indonesian movie company and Japan's Toho Company, Ltd., had fallen through sometime in 1953. Toho's producer Tomoyuki Tanaka needed something big to fill the gaping hole in the production schedule. On the plane ride back to Tokyo from Indonesia, he had an idea.

Speaking about this movie idea, Tanaka told the *Washington Post* in 1984, "The thesis is very simple. What if a dinosaur sleeping in the Southern Hemisphere had been awakened and transformed into a giant by the bomb? What if it attacked Tokyo?" The imagery of the creature's devastation was clearly taken from the destruction of Hiroshima and Nagasaki, two Japanese cities destroyed by U.S. atomic bombs in 1945.

Tanaka and special-effects master Eiji Tsuburaya very much wanted to make a monster movie in the American mold. Tanaka's simple idea of blending something the size of the 1933 movie monster King Kong with radiation was turned over to science-fiction

Godzilla was influenced by the 1953 American movie *The Beast from 20,000 Fathoms*. Both films were inspired by the fear caused by the invention of the atomic bomb in the 1940s, and the subsequent bombings of Hiroshima and Nagasaki.

author Shigeru Kayama. Kayama envisioned the monster as more of a threatening octopus. This initial idea, hewing closely to Ray Harryhausen's well-regarded 1953 release *The Beast from 20,000 Fathoms*, about an Arctic atomic test that awakened a slumbering dinosaur, quickly evolved from an octopus to a dinosaur. Tsuburaya's work on the creature was so influential that in later years, filmmakers

Steven Spielberg and George Lucas both publicly acknowledged his influence on their movies.

The story and production design of the film *Gojira* also evolved once Ishiro Honda was brought aboard as director. Honda used his eight years of military experience, including one year as a prisoner of war in China, to make the film darker, leading to its impact on the audience. Honda suggested that the creature's atomic breath symbolized the radiation fears of his people. He also helped reshape the initial story with screenwriter Takeo Murata, emphasizing the humans and de-emphasizing Gojira (Godzilla).

The man in the rubber suit, Haruo Nakajima, held the role as Gojira in Japan, from 1954 through 1972. There is an entire fan base for him, and the role of "man in the rubber suit" has become revered by cult film fanatics. Nakajima set the standard for any Japanese actor to hide himself under latex, foam rubber, and other appliances to do battle for either good or evil in films and television shows.

The first suit was constructed using a latex skin stuffed with bamboo and urethane foam. Several suits were made for each of the film's sequels because the materials never lasted. As a result, with each new movie, the design was constantly tweaked and modified. One aspect of the suit that has not changed is its color. Godzilla is charcoal gray, not green as has been seen in comic books, cartoon series, posters, and toys. Nakajima told *ABC News* in 1987, "It got very hot inside the suit. We measured it once and it was 60 degrees [Celsius, 140 degrees Fahrenheit]. It stank of sweat. I had to carry a 12-volt battery between my legs to move the eyes and mouth. Firecrackers were set inside the costume. I don't think today's actors would be able to perform under these conditions."

Honda also sought out music composer Akira Ifukube for the score. Ifukube was a professor of musical composition at Tokyo University and wanted to bring his own war experiences to the film. He created a haunting soundtrack that, like the costume, set a standard for all to follow. In all, he scored twenty-two Godzilla films and many more across all genres. It was Ifukube who designed the monster's distinctive roar. He simply rubbed a glove over a contrabass string and recorded the result.

As the suit was being constructed, Tokyo was rebuilt at one-twenty-fifth scale so the 165-foot-tall (50.3-meter-tall) monster had a city to smash. The size and scope of the creature and its destructive habits set the standard for all monster movies to come.

Japanese and American posters show Godzilla wreaking havoc on Tokyo. The original Japanese version of *Godzilla* was not released in the United States until 1994.

17

When *Gojira* opened in Japan on November 3, 1954, people were actually standing in line to buy tickets. The movie, which had cost Toho about $900,000 to make, was very profitable, finishing as the seventh top-grossing film of the year and winning the Japanese Film Technique Award for the special effects.

"After *Godzilla* was finished, movie journalists gave it a lot of negative reviews, so I was really worried about it," Tanaka told the fan magazine (fanzine) *G-Fan*. "So on opening day I went to Shibuya. What I saw there was a line as long as a snake, so inside I thought 'Alright!' I knew it was the line to see *Godzilla*, but I couldn't resist asking people what they were standing in line for. Over 9,691,000 people went to see it, and next to *King Kong vs. Godzilla*, it was the most popular at the box office of all Godzilla movies."

GOJIRA GOES TO HOLLYWOOD

Studios in Hollywood, California, noticed *Gojira*'s success, and a bidding war began to bring the film to local audiences in the United States. Embassy Pictures and producer Joseph E. Levine won the bid with the then-astounding sum of $25,000, and chose to shoot twenty minutes of new footage with director Terrell O. Morse. They reedited the film by removing forty minutes of story and adding dubbed voices, thus introducing an entirely new, purely American version to make it easier for audiences to identify with the story. Typical of the 1950s, foreign films were reedited, rescored, and then dubbed in English. They did not take the care to understand what the original producers had intended. It was at this point that Gojira became Godzilla (god-ZILL-ah), a name change that attempted to Americanize the Japanese name.

In 1956, in *Godzilla, King of the Monsters*, American movie-theater audiences saw one of their own, actor Raymond Burr, playing newspaper reporter Steve Martin and climbing out of the rubble from a city nearly destroyed by a radiation-breathing creature. The roles of Dr. Yamane and Dr. Serizawa, which were leading characters in the original Japanese film, were kept in the American version but as background characters. The events and actions in the reworked film are told from the viewpoint of American Steve Martin.

Raymond Burr starred as journalist Steve Martin in *Godzilla, King of the Monsters* (1956). He later achieved fame in television's drama series *Perry Mason* and *Ironside*.

THE SEQUELS

When Toho ordered a follow-up film, the creature terrorizing Tokyo was named Gigantis, because Gojira had been destroyed in the first film. Technically, it is this second creature that was featured in all subsequent films until *Godzilla 1985*. The film *Gojira no Gyakushu* (Counterattack of Godzilla) was rushed, released a mere six months after the original, and Honda was unavailable to direct it. Much as the first film reflected Japan's horror over the atomic age, the second film mirrored its reconstruction effort.

In the early 1960s, Godzilla returned from a seven-year layoff and battled Kong, the reigning monster from an earlier era. The story originated in the United States with Willis O'Brien, Kong's creator. When O'Brien could not find an American studio, he took the project to Toho. Toho replaced the script's original opponent with Godzilla and coproduced the movie with Universal Studios. With the larger budget and higher expectations, Godzilla made his color debut. Here, the Toho version is described by critics as a humorous and biting satire of corporate commerce in Japan. Universal totally missed the implied meaning of the movie, and its heavily edited version is seen as among the worst of the imports.

Honda's next effort was *Godzilla vs. the Thing*, pitting the monster against the butterfly-like creature Mothra. This was the final time Godzilla was seen as the sole menace to humanity, and it is considered by many critics to be the best of the series.

Henry G. Saperstein and his United Productions of America (UPA) saw the monsters' popularity and made a deal with Toho to import all the company's *kaiju*, or giant monster, movies. UPA's first import was *Godzilla vs. the Thing*, with

King Kong vs. Godzilla marks the first time that either monster appeared in color. Interestingly, it was the successful 1952 rerelease of *King Kong* in Japan that spawned the idea for *Godzilla*. Willis O'Brien originally wanted the movie to feature King Kong battling a Frankenstein-like monster made up of different animal parts.

Mothra's name in the title changed to the more generic name, Thing. By controlling Toho's American screen rights, UPA was also able to sell television rights to the films, which were enormously successful throughout the 1960s.

Despite the now global success of Godzilla films, the budget for each subsequent Toho film was being cut. The first cost-cutting measure was to recycle footage from other films. Next, less-detailed re-creations of Tokyo for Godzilla to stomp were made. Then the locale was moved from city to island as seen in *Godzilla vs. the Sea Monster*. Jun Fukuda did such a fine job directing *Sea Monster* that he was also at the helm for *Son of Godzilla*, which introduced Minya, the first of the several Godzilla offspring.

There were enough creatures available by 1969 for a battle royal, and *Destroy All Monsters* fit the bill perfectly. Audiences not only got to see the return of Honda to the director's chair, but they could also watch Godzilla, Minya, Mothra, Rodan, Angilas, Gorosaurus, and Manda trash cities around the world.

Despite the lure of all the monsters in one film at the box office, ticket sales continued to decline. Toho felt that the only way to sustain the series was to continue trimming the budget and aim the films at younger, less critical audiences. The lowest point came immediately with *Godzilla's Revenge*, released in the United States in 1971, which recycled most of its special-effects footage and reduced the monster fights to dream sequences.

Fukuda had replaced Honda as series director, and he disliked the job, preferring to

Godzilla vs. the Sea Monster **(1966) was the first of six** *Godzilla* **films directed by Jun Fukuda. The film was originally written to star King Kong and was called** *Operation Robinson Crusoe.*

Destroy All Monsters (1969) features a total of eleven monsters, the most for any Godzilla film. The movie also marks the last time all four original key players in the Godzilla franchise—director Ishiro Honda, producer Tomoyuki Tanaka, musician Akira Ifukube, and special-effects supervisor Eiji Tsuburaya—worked together on a Godzilla film.

shoot comedies. Fukuda's lighter touch did not appeal to diehard fans nor did the continued supersizing of the monster's intelligence as he literally planned his attacks to save the world. Fukuda was replaced by Yoshimitsu Banno, who also cowrote the story for *Godzilla vs. the Smog Monster*, which was released in the United States in 1972. (The only time Godzilla flies is in this movie.)

GODZILLA'S OFFSPRING

Most movie audiences think Godzilla had just one child, a belief reinforced by the appearance of Godzooky in the American animated series airing on ABC in the 1970s.

The first child, Minya, was introduced in *Son of Godzilla* in the 1960s, and remained at Godzilla's side through the subsequent features. During the late 1970s, the child was dubbed Godzooky in the American animated series.

After the series was relaunched with *Godzilla 1985*, it was eight years before a child became part of the story again, which happened with *Godzilla vs. Mechagodzilla*. Producer Tomoyuki Tanaka was unhappy with Baby Godzilla's look and had him redesigned, and Tanaka renamed him Little Godzilla, in the following *Godzilla vs. Space Godzilla*. In *Godzilla vs. Destroyer*, he became known as Godzilla Jr., having grown to 98 feet (30 m) tall.

Eventually, Junior was seemingly killed, but radiation emanating from Godzilla himself acted as an infusion of new energy and Junior was revived. He also grew to full adult size and was last seen wandering Japan with his father.

Son of Godzilla (1967) introduced Minya, an offspring of Godzilla who would appear in many films in the series. This movie was the second title in the franchise to be sold directly to TV (the first was *Godzilla vs. the Sea Monster*).

Fukuda wanted to make his return film, *Godzilla vs. Gigan*, another monster fest, but as the script developed, it was simplified. To cut costs, footage is recycled as is the musical score, for the first time. The low-budget approach of the 1972 film continued in the following year's *Godzilla vs. Megalon*, with the new monster being a leftover idea from the previous film.

Fukuda's swan song in the series was the twentieth-anniversary epic, *Godzilla vs. the Cosmic Monster*. With Fukuda gone, Tanaka brought back Honda and a return to the darker tones of the earlier films. Their reunion project in 1975 was a direct sequel, *Terror of Mechagodzilla*. Tanaka also brought back Ifukube to write his first new score since *Destroy All Monsters*.

Despite the return of all this talent, the box-office receipts were not encouraging, and Toho finally decided to let the monster slumber. By now, Tanaka recognized that the endless *Godzilla vs.* movies and lightening of the tone had been a mistake. When the creature returned to the screen, Toho was going to have a fresh start.

A NEW BEGINNING

Tanaka knew what he needed to do. He got the studio's support, and on December 26, 1983, announced that Godzilla would be back. As Tanaka crafted a new story, he reimagined the creature as about 65 feet (20 m) taller, more violent, and a greater threat to humanity. These ideas did not seem encouraging as both Honda and Ifukube refused to participate.

Instead, Tanaka asked Kohji Hashimoto to be the new director. The new rubber suit redesigned Godzilla's look. Coupled with a script that was a modern-day consideration of the nuclear question, the film was an enormous success. Avco Embassy picked up American rights and decided the remake needed actor Raymond Burr back. Burr told the *Washington Post* in 1986, "When they asked me to do it the second time, I said, 'Certainly,' and everybody thought I was out of my mind. But it wasn't the large sum of money. It was the fact that first of all, I kind of liked Godzilla, and where do you get the opportunity to play yourself 30 years later?"

Interestingly, *Godzilla 1985* was the last Toho import to receive an official U.S. release. Film clubs, film festivals, and the like have had screenings of the subsequent Japanese release, and all twenty-seven of the *Godzilla* films are available on DVD or VHS.

Tanaka continued to produce movies, hoping for edgier fare. However, Toho preferred making movies that appealed to children, especially because the drop at the box office had yet to stop.

By the early 1990s, Toho had sold American remake rights to Tri-Star and expected to fold its version of the Godzilla character. Instead, Tri-Star's development of the film stalled, as most projects do in Hollywood. As each project release date came and went, Toho returned to production, cranking out annual releases expecting each to be the last.

Godzilla 1985 was the last Toho import to receive an official U.S. release. The remake featured Raymond Burr reprising his role as Steve Martin. It was also supposed to include Akhiko Hirata as Dr. Serizawa, but the actor died of cancer just before filming began.

THE AMERICAN GODZILLA

When Tri-Star finally had everything in place, Toho decided to kill Godzilla for good in *Godzilla vs. Destroyer*. In the back of the studio's mind, it figured it had an out with a planned series of films featuring Godzilla's offspring, now an adult, but those plans never materialized. The 1995 film brought Akira Ifukube out of retirement to compose the score. Fittingly, a new creature, dubbed Destroyer, was created as a result of the Oxygen Destroyer used to subdue Godzilla in the very first feature, forty years earlier.

In 1998, director Roland Emmerich and producer and writer Dean Devlin made an American interpretation of the classic Godzilla story, redesigning the creature's appearance and setting the story in New York City. The $125 million Tri-Star production of *Godzilla* was roundly criticized as a creative failure and was seen as a box-office disappointment despite earning $136,023,813 in its initial release. Fans rejected the interpretation, and it is not considered a legitimate part of the Godzilla series. After the American version failed to be a success, Toho cranked up production once more.

The most interesting reinterpretation of Godzilla came in 2001, from director Shusuke Kaneko, noted for his earlier work on a Gamera trilogy. (Gamera is a giant flying turtle.) *Godzilla, Mothra, King Ghidorah: The Giant Monsters' General Offensive* depicted Godzilla not as a beast unleashed through nuclear horror, but a manifestation of those who died in war. The other monsters were seen as guardian spirits, opposing the wrath of the dead.

CHAPTER **3**

REFLECTION ON SOCIETY

Gojira was released in 1954, and was considered the best monster movie of its kind, literally creating a new genre of moviemaking in Japan known as *kaiju*, which means "giant monster." People also saw it as a commentary on the nuclear horrors of World War II, which had ended just nine years earlier. It was a smash success at the Japanese box office.

In 1991, director Honda told the fanzine *G-Fan*, "The number one question concerning [*Gojira*] was the fear connected to what was then known as the atomic bomb, in the original film. At the time, I think there was an ability to grasp 'a thing of absolute terror,' as Shigeru Kayama himself called it. When I directed that film, in terms of society at the time, it was a surprising movie with all its special effects but, actually, when I returned from the war and passed through Hiroshima, there was a heavy atmosphere—a fear the earth was already coming to an end. That became my basis."

APOCALYPTIC THREAT

Godzilla represents the beginning of a modern-day myth, owing nothing to any Japanese lore, making the monster unique. Instead, he was created to address lingering concerns of atomic weaponry. On May 2, 2004, Terrence Rafferty wrote in the *New York Times* that the first film "is extraordinarily solemn, full of earnest discussions about how to respond to the apocalyptic threat—one thoughtful scientist . . . argues that the monster should not be killed but studied for clues to surviving the effects of radiation. . . .

"The most peculiar thing about Godzilla as a metaphor for the bomb is the creature's simultaneous status as a legendary beast of Japanese islanders' mythology: surely a more precise representation of the disaster that befell the country at the end of the Second World War would be an agent of destruction from far away, unheard of even in legend, not this native, almost familiar, monster. Is Godzilla, then, also on some subterranean level a metaphor for Japan's former imperial ambitions, which finally unleashed the retaliatory fury that leveled its cities?"

The film succeeded in Japan because it spoke to contemporary fears within an entertaining framework. The fact that Japanese ingenuity defeated the creature was a chance to show hope to a people desperate for it.

In other countries, though, the film succeeded because no one had seen anything quite like Godzilla. Movie monsters of the 1950s tended to be large-headed creatures from other worlds, supersized ants, or creatures with fangs and

This photograph shows Hiroshima one month after the atom bomb was dropped on the city. The destruction wrought by the bomb, and the lingering effects of radiation, caused fear throughout the world, but was especially devastating in Japan. *Godzilla* spoke to the fears of Japanese society while also providing escapist entertainment.

the occasional tentacle. A monster based on ancient dinosaurs was original as was its atomic breath.

Honda told *Asiaweek*, "Believe it or not, we had no plans for a sequel and naively hoped that the end of Godzilla was going to coincide with the end of nuclear testing." Instead, nations around the world continued to test atomic weaponry for the next several decades.

By creating Godzilla to reflect the fears and concerns of Japanese society in the mid-twentieth century, they continued to evolve the myth to reflect the times. Much as the movies reflected Cold War concerns, *Godzilla vs. the Sea Monster* (1966) most closely mirrored the spy movies that were popular in the 1960s. In fact, James Bond's *You Only Live Twice* (1967) had just filmed in Japan, and its influence was keenly seen in *Sea Monster* as the human interactions between monster attacks had an unusual snap to them.

NO LONGER A REFLECTION

As the 1970s arrived, the world was concerned with air pollution. Consequently, Godzilla had to stop the Smog Monster. But by then, nearly twenty years after his introduction, Godzilla had been solidified into an entertaining monster, at times lovable, at times to be feared. Toho's personnel stopped being topical and went back to the tried and true formula of pitting Godzilla against new threats while teaming with a growing array of fellow creatures.

Godzilla as a reflection of Japanese society may be one reason it failed to be successfully adapted by Hollywood. Author Douglas Rushkoff wrote in 1998, "The *Godzilla* movie myth emerged from a nation that had survived a nuclear holocaust. The monster was less the enemy of the Japanese than he was the embodiment of their own defeated spirit, rising like a giant sumo wrestler to avenge the carnage wrought by Western technology. He is not nature, but a man-made

Godzilla vs. the Smog Monster (1972) was the first film in the series since *Godzilla vs. the Thing* (1964) to carry a strong social message. It is also the only Godzilla movie in which the monster flies. He does so by firing his atomic breath on the ground and propelling himself backward.

freak of nature, with his own personality and free will. This is why he failed so miserably when cast in a role equivalent to the mindless tornado in the American-style natural disaster movie *Twister*."

CHAPTER 4

GODZILLA, THE PHENOMENON

Over the years, Toho's filmmakers kept changing their minds about how large and how powerful the monster Godzilla was. They also periodically strayed from the original tenets of the Godzilla story and created fresh stories that stemmed from the first Japanese film.

The first set of films involves one timeline and continuing story elements, known as *Showa* (first generation). They are marked by the threat of the monster. The next major timeline is known as the *Heisei* (second generation) series and starts with the original *Godzilla* but ignores the story lines from every movie until *Godzilla 1985*. This movie, released in 1984, restored Godzilla to being a menace to the world. The *Heisei* series of films lasted until 1995's *Godzilla vs. Destroyer*. Since 1998, the new timeline is simply called "the new series" although some fans argue that the movies since *Godzilla 2000* can be considered part of the *Heisei* series.

Godzilla was quickly brought to America with successful results, so Toho managed to

Godzilla 2000 **used a completely computer-generated Godzilla, the first time that was ever done in the series. It was also the first to feature a monster that had green skin. In the other films, Godzilla is charcoal gray.**

sell the film to most major countries around the world. Just as the Americans used their nation's actors to film scenes to adjust the film for local audiences, Germany changed the story line so that the monsters sent after Godzilla were created by Dr. Frankenstein.

AMERICA EMBRACES THE MONSTER

In 1969, Marv Newland made the simply animated one-minute short *Bambi Meets Godzilla* that remains a staple in a variety of "the best of video" collections. Bambi is seen eating grass during the majority of the film. In the final second, a giant scaled foot crushes the deer.

Godzilla's popularity was such that in the 1970s, Godzilla was deemed safe enough for children of all ages and received an ABC television network's Saturday morning animated series produced by Hanna-Barbera. It was successful enough to last two seasons. Immediately after Tri-Star's *Godzilla* (1998) disaster, a forty-episode animated series was launched in September 1998. The story line picked up immediately after the film ended. The series, produced for the FOX network by Centropolis, ran for two seasons and was considered by fans a superior effort to the American film in terms of story, characterization, and execution.

In 1977, Marvel Comics had some success with its own interpretation of *Godzilla*. The comic, written by Doug Moench and drawn by Herb Trimpe, lasted only twenty-four issues and was canceled when Toho became frustrated with the approach to its creation, not due to declining sales. The monster fought the army, other beasts, and even Marvel's heroic Avengers.

Tri-Star originally planned two sequels to *Godzilla* (1998), but decided against the idea when the film turned out to be a critical and commercial disaster.

This Saturday morning cartoon series from the 1970s, called *The Godzilla Power Hour*, showed a kinder, gentler Godzilla than is usually seen in the movies. The story line featured a research crew that investigates strange occurrences and often needs to summon Godzilla for help when it encounters dangerous beasts.

Godzilla returned to comics in 1988, this time at Dark Horse, which presented his adventures in a miniseries and a number of one-shots. (A one-shot is a single-issue story featuring the title character.) One of the most unusual of these pitted him against basketball legend Charles Barkley. Numerous comics artists who grew up with *Godzilla* films clamored to illustrate the monster, making the books a treat to read.

In the early 1980s, the United States tried its own version of *Godzilla*. The studio 20th Century Fox planned a $25 million production in 3-D, with director Steve Miner. The great dinosaur artist William Stout was brought onboard to design the look of the film's character, but after months of planning, the film was scuttled. Stout subsequently went on to write one of the episodes of the animated *Godzilla*, based on the 1998 Tri-Star production.

ABC News broadcast a report in 2003 on Godzilla's enduring appeal. One Japanese citizen told reporter Mark Simkin, "Godzilla is special for Japan. When people look at Japan, they think of Mount Fuji, geisha, and Godzilla."

The producer who brought most of the Godzilla movies to America, Henry Saperstein, before he died, mused to *G-Fan* on why the monster Godzilla endures. "I think Godzilla's an icon that has been established, and that Godzilla will continue to remain an icon with the public. The public has been going through all these periods of reality being a little too much to take, it's too harsh. So the fantasy of something that's bigger than life . . . Godzilla's a morality play; good guys against bad guys, and Godzilla, like the Lone Ranger, coming forth, reluc-tantly, to strike down the bad guys, is something that appeals to the psyche of a public that is beset by prob-lems of poverty and homelessness and AIDS, and government pressures and the stock market and all those other things. It's kind of nice to sit back, kick off your shoes, open your belt and watch Godzilla do his thing . . . it feels good."

This photograph shows a crew member filming Toho's twenty-fourth *Godzilla* movie in 2000. Interest in the Godzilla phenomenon was such that when Toho organized a weeklong tour for fans to observe the filming of the movie, 1,500 people applied to attend.

GOLDEN ANNIVERSARY

In October 2004, for the monster's fiftieth anniversary, the Center for East Asian Studies at the University of Kansas held a symposium, which included a wide range of disciplines, entitled "In Godzilla's Footsteps: Japanese Pop Culture Icons on the Global Stage." The symposium participants considered the Godzilla films and how they influenced and were influenced by postwar Japanese culture, including the effect of Japanese popular culture around the world.

Toshio Takahashi, professor of literature at the University of Rochester, told *ABC News'* Mark Simkin in 2003, "The first Godzilla movie was aimed at adults. Since then, though, Godzilla's personality has changed. It's become a protector of humans and the movies have appealed more to children. The popularity of Godzilla is starting to fade. A severe situation is coming."

Toho announced the December 4, 2004, release in Japan of *Godzilla: Final Wars*. A United States release followed in 2005. Toho's Shogo Tomiyama said, as reported in the *Kyodo News*, "We have done all we can to showcase Godzilla, including using computer-graphics technology. And yet we haven't attracted new fans. So we will make the 50th anniversary film something special, a best-of-the-best, and then end it for now. I don't think there will be another movie for at least five or maybe 10 years. I would like to pour all the know-how of the last 50 years into this commemorative movie and make it the best one."

Godzilla: Final Wars was reported to feature Godzilla along with a series of other monsters, including Mothra, Rodan, Angilas, Gigan, Manda, Hedorah, Kumunga, Kamakaris, Ebirah, Minya, King Seesar, and the brand-new Monster X. Director Ryuhei Kitamura has cast Masahiro Matsuoka as the soldier with a superhuman body who battles the monsters in the film and Rei Kikukawa as the molecular biologist who studies the monsters. The monsters will wreak havoc in New York City, Paris, Shanghai, and, of course, Tokyo.

FILMOGRAPHY

Godzilla, King of the Monsters
(1956). Directed by Ishiro Honda, with
new film inserted, edited, and dubbed under
the direction of Terry Morse. Hydrogen bomb
tests awaken and mutate an ancient creature, who
shows his displeasure to the inhabitants of Tokyo.

Counterattack of Godzilla (1959). Another of Godzilla's
species is discovered, this one engaged in battle with the
monster Angilas. They then take their battle to Japan.

King Kong vs. Godzilla (1963). When a pharmaceutical
company captures King Kong and brings him to Japan for
a promotion, Godzilla also turns up.

Godzilla vs. the Thing (1964). A greedy developer finds one
of Mothra's eggs and disturbs Godzilla's slumber.

Ghidorah, the Three-Headed Monster (1965). Ghidorah
arrives via meteor and threatens Japan.

Godzilla vs. Monster Zero (1970). Aliens from Planet X ask
for Godzilla and Rodan to come help them stop a being
called King Ghidorah.

Godzilla vs. the Sea Monster (1966). The Red Bamboo, a
terrorist group, wants to rule the world and have mas-
tered Ebirah to do its bidding.

Son of Godzilla (1967). A weather experiment goes out of
control, turning mantises into monsters.

Destroy All Monsters (1969). Aliens use their technology to
control Earth's monsters.

Godzilla's Revenge (1971). A boy imagines life on Monster
Island.

Godzilla vs. the Smog Monster (1972). Earth's runaway pollution problems create a new monster, Hedorah.

Godzilla vs. Gigan (1978). Aliens want to conquer Earth with the aid of Gigan and King Ghidorah.

Godzilla vs. Megalon (1976). Seatopia uses the giant beetle Megalon and Gigan to destroy surface-dwelling humans.

Godzilla vs. Mechagodzilla (1977). A mechanical Godzilla is built by aliens to stall Godzilla as they attempt to conquer Earth.

The Terror of Godzilla (1979). Mechagodzilla is rebuilt by aliens and a mad scientist teams the robot with a monster, Titanosaurus.

Godzilla 1985 (1985). Hydrogen bomb tests awaken and mutate an ancient creature, who shows his displeasure to the inhabitants of Tokyo.

GLOSSARY

box office The office where movie tickets are sold. It is also the amount of money taken in by each movie theater, as in box-office receipts. Movie studios take a percentage of each ticket sale, varying by film.

director The director is considered the head man or woman of a film. He or she has a say in the shape of the story, the actors who bring the characters to life, the look of the costumes and sets, editing, and score. The director takes an idea or a vision and brings it to life using selected resources before and behind the camera.

dub To record voices and sound effects over an existing film.

editor The person who takes all the raw footage and starts assembling it into a coherent whole. Usually, a director shoots the same scene from several angles, and an editor selects the best angle to help tell the story.

paleontologist A scientist who studies the life of past geological periods as known from fossil remains.

producer The person in charge of a movie's production in all matters, except for the creative efforts of the director.

score The music composition used to help create a specific mood and feeling for each scene and the film as a whole.

screenwriter The writer of screenplays, which are the scripts and shooting directions of a story for film production.

special effects These are the visual and sound effects used in movies that are created when they are not naturally available, ranging from giant monsters to explosions.

FOR MORE INFORMATION

Academy of Motion Picture Arts
    and Sciences
8949 Wilshire Boulevard
Beverly Hills, CA 90211-1972
(310) 247-3000
Web site: http://www.oscars.org

American Film Institute
The John F. Kennedy Center for the Performing Arts
Washington, DC 20566
(202) 833-AFIT (2348)
Web site: http://www.AFI.com

G-Fan
Box 3468
Steinbach, Manitoba
Canada, R0A 2A0
(204) 326-7754
Web site: http://www.g-fan.com

WEB SITES

Due to the changing nature of Internet links, the Rosen
Publishing Group, Inc., has developed an online list of Web
sites related to the subject of this book. This site is updated
regularly. Please use this link to access the list:

http://www.rosenlinks.com/famm/mego

FOR FURTHER READING

Aylesworth, Thomas G. *Movie Monsters*. Philadelphia: J. B. Lippincott Company, 1975.

Cain, Dana. *Collecting Japanese Movie Monsters*. Norfolk, VA: Antique Trade Books, 1998.

Cerasini, Marc. *Godzilla at World's End*. New York: Random House Children's Books, 1998.

Cerasini, Marc. *Godzilla Vs. the Robot Monsters*. New York: Random House Children's Books, 1998.

Cohen, Daniel. *Hollywood Dinosaur*. New York: Simon & Schuster Children's Publishing, 1987.

Cohen, Daniel. *Science Fiction's Greatest Monsters*. New York: Simon & Schuster Children's Publishing, 1986.

Daniels, Stephen. *Movie Monsters*. Mahwah, NJ: Watermill Press, 1980.

Hollings, Ken. *Destroy All Monsters*. London: Marion Boyars Publishers, 2001.

Lees, J. D. *The Official Godzilla Compendium*. New York: Random House, 1998.

Marrero, Robert, and Margot Winick, eds. *Godzilla-King of the Movie Monsters: An Illustrated Guide to Japanese Monster Movies*. Key West, FL: Fantasma Books, 1996.

The Official Godzilla Movie Fact Book. Adapted by Dawn Margolis. New York: Scholastic Books, Inc., 1998.

Powers, Tom. *Movie Monsters*. Minneapolis: Lerner Publishing Group, 1989.

Quackenbush, Robert, and Kathleen Tucker, eds. *Movie Monsters and Their Masters: The Birth of the Horror Film*. Morton Grove, IL: Albert Whitman & Company, 1980.

BIBLIOGRAPHY

"Godzilla and Other Toho Studios Movies."
Retrieved May 28, 2004 (http://www.westol.com/
~schneidr/dke/mgodz.htm).

Hood, Robert. "A Potted History of Godzilla." Retrieved May 28,
2004 (http://www.roberthood.net/obsesses/godzilla.htm).

Kalat, David. *A Critical History and Filmography of Toho's
Godzilla Series*. Jefferson, NC: McFarland and Company,
Inc., 1997.

Rafferty, Terrence. "The Monster That Morphed into a
Metaphor." *New York Times*, May 2, 2004.

Roberto, John Rocco. "Godzilla and the Second World War. A
Study of the Allegorical Meaning in Godzilla Raids Again."
Retrieved May 24, 2004 (http://www.dalekempire.com/
GodzillaWWII.html).

Roberto, John Rocco. "Japan, Godzilla and the Atomic Bomb.
A Study into the Effects of the Atomic Bomb on Japanese
Pop Culture." Retrieved May 24, 2004 (http://www.
dalekempire.com/JapanGodzillaAtomic Bomb.html).

Rushkoff, Douglas. "The Godzilla Factor." Retrieved May 26,
2004 (http://www.rushkoff.com/cgi-
bin/columns/display.cgi/the_godzilla_factor).

INDEX

ABOUT THE AUTHOR

Robert Greenberger is a senior editor at DC Comics. In addition, he writes *Star Trek* novels and numerous nonfiction books. *Godzilla* scared the heck out of him in the 1960s, but he claims to have gotten over it.

PHOTO CREDITS

Cover, pp. 1, 4, 8, 10, 12, 14, 15, 17, 19, 21, 22, 23, 24, 27, 29, 33, 34, 35, 36, 37 © The Everett Collection; p. 31 © Bettmann/Corbis; p. 39 © AP/Wide World Photos.

Designer: Thomas Forget; Editor: Kathy Kuhtz Campbell